The Power of Insight

Thomas Troward's Discoveries in India

The Power of Insight

Thomas Troward's
Discoveries in India

told by Ruth L. Miller

illustrated by Martha Shonkwiler

A *Paths of Power* book
from

WISEWOMAN PRESS

The Power of Insight: Thomas Troward's Discoveries in
India

By Ruth L. Miller
© 2012

Illustrated by Martha Shonkwiler

WiseWoman Press
Vancouver, WA

ISBN: 978-0-945385-44-8

Imagine growing up in a country where you have lots of servants and a nanny who speaks a strange ancient language and practices an equally ancient religion...

Imagine being sent away from your family to another country to go to school and being unhappy for years before finally making life work...

Imagine being given a job back in another part of the country you remember from childhood and using that language you learned from the servants to learn about the ancient religion you saw when you were a child—and lots of others, too...

Imagine seeing things and hearing things that all your teachers said were impossible...

That's what happened to Thomas Troward, and he figured out how it all worked!

CONTENTS

1

Childhood in Ceylon

Thomas Troward was born on the South Seas island of Ceylon (known today as Sri Lanka) in 1847. His British parents, Albany and Frederica Troward, were from Middlesex, back in the heart of England. His father was a full colonel in the British-Indian Army who had served in India most of his life. He was transferred to Ceylon just before his son was born, and so it was there that Thomas spent the first years of his life.

Sri Lanka is a tropical island off the coast of India, with lots of sand and palm trees along the beaches and jungle in the highlands. When Thomas was alive, it was a colony of the British Empire. British soldiers and government workers managed the economic and political life of the country, and trained local people to be clerks and supervisors.

Like most British children in India and Ceylon, Thomas lived in a community of British families in a big, open house, with lots of rooms and lots of local people as servants. He had a nurse, who would have been called a nanny in England, but in the British colonies of India and Ceylon was called an *ayyah*. She helped him dress and made sure he ate properly and rested properly and read him stories or sing to him at night and took him outside to play each day. And like most British children of his day, he only saw his parents for a few minutes in the late afternoon or evening each day and for a few hours on Sundays and holidays, when they went to church and visited other British and European families in the area.

From his *ayyah*, Thomas learned to love the sound of the ancient language that she spoke. It was related to *Hindi* and *Sanskrit*, the ancient language from which English and all the European languages evolved.

People in Ceylon and India were very religious. Thomas was fascinated when he watched her pray at the little altar in her closet. And every day he heard the men who worked in the house go outside and pray as the sun rose and again as the sun set. He loved the sound of it and was fascinated by how different it was from the prayers and hymns he learned in church.

On visits into town, Thomas got to see wandering Buddhist monks in their bright orange robes, as they went along with their offering bowls, talking with anyone who cared to listen about the life and teachings of the Buddha. He also saw great processions, as people danced and sang their way through the streets for a Hindu holy day or religious ceremony.

Sometimes he would get to visit the marketplace in town with his *ayyah* or another of the servants. So many people! So much noise and confusion!

He much preferred the peace he felt when they went to the beach and he could watch the ocean. He loved to watch the waves, and see the sunlight reflected on the water. Sometimes he would watch people as they sat on the beach painting pictures—and he realized he wanted to do that, too.

At School in England

When he was about 12 years old Thomas' father told him that it was time he learned how to be a proper Englishman. He would have to go to England and get a good education so he could have a good life.

4

Thomas had never been in England, but of course he'd heard about it all his life, so he was curious. So he was more excited than scared when he and some other children were escorted onto a big sailing ship for the journey.

First they sailed to India, where they changed ships. Thomas was fascinated by all the activity at the port. Then they boarded the big, ocean-going vessel with lots of sails that would carry them around Africa and up along the coast of Europe, all the way to the land the children had all been told was "home."

It was a very long trip, and sometimes it seemed like they'd never get to see land again, but Thomas was happy whenever he could stand on deck and watch the sky and water, and the way the early morning light was different from the afternoon light. He sometimes saw dolphins or porpoises playing alongside or out in front of the ship, and that really pleased him.

Finally, they could see the famous White Cliffs of Dover that his parents had told him to watch for. They were almost there!

Although it was still summer, England is much cooler than Sri Lanka, and all the children realized that they would really need the strange clothes their parents had sent with them. Those sweaters and long socks and heavy woolen jackets suddenly made sense!

Like most boys in those days, whether they had been born in England or another part of the British Empire, Thomas attended the boarding school his father had attended. It was called Burmshtead School (which is written as Beckhamstead, like the label on a bottle of "worshter" sauce says Worcestershire).

Sadly, even though it was a good school, with all the important courses, he just wasn't interested in what they were teaching. Instead, he enjoyed walking in the beautiful green countryside, He was not nearly as interested in arithmetic and spelling and such, as he was in the way the light and shadow fell on the leaves and grasses outside, and how the sky was reflected in the streams and rivers.

That lasted until he turned 16. That's when he went to Helford College, a small school in the part of England called Jersey.

There, Thomas learned to love to study. He especially loved to read the poetry and novels and essays of the great writers of past centuries. Shakespeare and Francis Bacon were two of his favorites, but he also liked reading the famous Roman writers: Cicero, Livy, and Marcellus—as well as the great German philosopher Johann von Goethe and the American writer Ralph Waldo Emerson, among many others. He also learned to love the beauty of the Bible.

So, in 1865, at the age of 18, he graduated from college with gold medal honors in literature. He wanted to be an artist but realized he needed to earn a living, so he decided to study Law for a career. His grandfather was a lawyer and he admired the essays of some of the great Roman and British lawyers. He was also fascinated by the laws of Moses in the Bible, so he thought he might be able to do the job.

Thomas graduated from law school and apprenticed as a clerk in the London courts. He did well, but he realized he was homesick for the tropics of Ceylon and India. He decided, at age 22, in 1869, he returned to India and took the difficult Indian Civil Service Examination.

One of the subjects on that exam was metaphysics (the study of how things came to be and why they are the way we experience them). Sadly, this was the very last subject on his list to prepare for the exam, and he hadn't really studied it.

Still, as always, he gave it his best, answering the questions as clearly as he could.

What he wrote surprised the Oxford professor who graded the exam, and he asked Thomas where he got his ideas. When Thomas told him he'd made them up, the professor told him that the world would very likely hear more from him in the years to come. And now we know that professor was right!

2

An Englishman in India

Thomas was immediately appointed to the post of Assistant Commissioner in the Northwest part of India called the Punjab and just a few years later, was promoted to Divisional Judge. He lived and worked there, at the foot of the Himalayan mountains for the next 25 years.

Soon after he received his first appointment, Thomas married his first wife. Together, they had three children, who lived with them there in the same way Thomas had lived with his parents, growing up in Ceylon.

The life of an Englishman in that part of India during those years was fascinating. They lived in houses that were similar to English cottages, but with large openings in the walls instead of windows, and doorways that had openings above and below, so whatever breezes there might be could flow through. Indian beds were also designed for good air flow: instead of a mattress on box springs or a foam pad on a platform, people in India slept on rope netting strung on wooden frames called *charpoys*, with light, open-weave sheets and blankets and mosquito netting around them.

English families also had servants—lots of them. The British government said that the practice of having servants gave employment to the local villagers. They also made life in the hot climate almost comfortable for people who were used to the much cooler weather of England—and were used to having things like flush toilets and running water and ice without having to lift and carry them!

Even so, it was a difficult life for many—too much was too different from "back home." And those who didn't adjust either returned to England or, sadly, became ill and passed away.

But for the people who did adjust (and Thomas was one of these!), there were all kinds of interesting things to see and learn and discover in this ancient land.

There were temples and mosques and palaces and ancient monasteries with wonderful art and libraries full of ancient manuscripts. There were statues and shrines everywhere, with beautiful offerings of food and flowers.

Every day, in the market place, holy men would sit and tell stories or demonstrate how their practice of yoga had given them control over their bodies. They might sleep on a bed of nails or entice a cobra or tiger to behave in a loving way. While they did these things, their students, called *chelas* would roam through the crowds gathering offerings of food and money.

On holy days there were processions through the streets, as there had been in Ceylon when Thomas was a boy, with singing and dancing and drums and trumpets and flowers strewn everywhere. Weddings lasted for days and involved whole towns, with feasting singing and dancing late into the night.

And, in the poor farming villages, women wrapped in colorful *saris* would carry water from the well in big pots on their heads or shoulders. And they would gather wheat from the fields, carrying huge bundles on their heads, and cook big pots of lentil stew on open fires in the center of the floor of their stone or mud houses to feed their families.

Stories from the Punjab

Thomas later told his British friends some stories of those early years. One of them is a true ghost story and tells us a lot about the way he lived and how he came to feel about death.

> About the year 1873, when I was a young Assistant Commissioner in the Punjab, I was ordered to a small up-country station that I'll call Akalpur. My wife and I moved into the Assistant Commissioner's bungalow there and had our beds (*charboys*) placed side by side in one of the rooms.

That night, as I was going to sleep, my wife was sitting up in her bed next to me, reading. I was awakened suddenly by the sound of a shot. In the dark, I lit the candle beside my bed and saw my wife sitting in the same position she had been.

"Take me away. Take me into another room," she exclaimed.

"Why, what is the matter?" I said.

"Did you not see it?" she asked.

"See what?"

"Don't stop to ask any questions," she replied, "Get me out of this room at once! I can't stay here another minute!"

I saw that she was very frightened, so I had the servants help us move our beds to a room on the other side of the house. Then she told me what she'd seen.

"I was sitting reading as you saw me, when looking round, I saw the figure of an Englishman standing close by my bedside, a fine looking man with a large fair moustache and dressed in a grey suit. I was so surprised that I could not speak, and we remained looking at each other for about a minute. Then he bent over me and said, 'Don't be afraid,' and then there was a shot and everything was in darkness."

"My dear girl, you must have fallen asleep over your book and been dreaming," I said.

"No. I was wide awake," she insisted; "you were asleep, but I was wide awake the whole time. But you heard the shot, did you not?"

"Yes," I replied. "That is what woke me—some one must have fired a shot outside."

"But why should anyone be shooting in our garden at nearly midnight?"

It certainly seemed strange, but it was the only explanation I could think of. So we agreed to differ. Nonetheless, out of respect for her feelings, I had our beds moved to another room in the house where we tried to sleep.

The next morning the owner of the bungalow, an old widow lady, came by to see if there were anything she could do for us. After thanking her, my wife said, "I expect you will laugh at me, but I cannot help telling you there's something strange about the bungalow," and went on to share what she'd seen.

Instead of laughing, the old lady looked more and more serious as my wife told her tale and asked to be shown exactly where the image had appeared. On seeing it, she exclaimed, "This is the most wonderful thing I've ever heard of! Eighteen years ago my bed was on the very spot where yours was last night and I was lying in it, too ill to move, when my husband, whom you have described most accurately, stood where you saw him and died."

Twenty years later, I was sharing this story with a colonel who knew the man, and he said to me, "Do you know what the last words he said to his wife were?"

"No," was my reply.

"The very same words he spoke to your wife," said the colonel.

Needless to say, these confirmations of my wife's experience have led me to study this sort of phenomenon ever since. And, over the years, I've met many trustworthy people who've told me that they too have personally had such experiences.

This was the first of many events like this in Thomas' life. In fact, years later he would become famous for his work explaining how such things could happen.

While in India, Thomas learned the language of the country. He'd learned to speak a little *Urdu* from his *Ayya* and the common language of India, Hindi, when he was a child. In the Punjab, though, he had to be able to speak and understand *Urdu* and to read Hindi and Sanskrit, as well.

Being able to speak their language meant he could help the people in his district more effectively. That meant he could make decisions that would benefit all parties—and he became known as an unusually fair and understanding judge.

It also made it possible for him to read the books that were important to the people he was helping. So he studied all of the bibles of that part of the world, including the Muslim Holy Koran, the Hindu scriptures (called *Vedas* and *Upanishads)* and the books of Raja Yoga.

Then, in order to compare these works with his beloved Bible, he studied the ancient biblical Hebrew, which has many similarities to Sanskrit.

Speaking the language also meant he could ask questions of some of those holy men who taught in the market place. From them he learned about the ancient scriptures and about the methods these men used to make their bodies do things most of us can't even imagine. Besides sleeping on beds of nails, they could live on almost no food or water, and even be buried in a box for several days and come out smiling! He also learned about the difference between understanding something with the mind and practicing something so long that it becomes a part of us.

Once, when he was deep in this study, a vision came to him that he would develop a system of thought that gave peace of mind as well as physical health and happiness to everyone in the world. He had no idea how that might happen, but he was willing to do whatever might move his ideas forward.

Sadly, Mrs. Troward, who had shared so many wonderful experiences with him, died there in India, along with their three children. Thomas was devastated and buried himself in his work and studies for years. It wasn't unusual in those days for a whole family to come down with a fever or flu and not recover, but it was still terribly painful. And Thomas felt it deeply.

3

A New Life in England

Time heals all wounds, however, and Thomas married a second time. His second wife, Sarah Ann (known as "Annie"), returned with him to England and helped in the publishing of his works. They had three children: two daughters, whom they named Ruth and Budeia, and a son they called Rupert.

All his life, in and around studying, working, and raising a family, Thomas had always, in his heart, thought of himself as an artist. He still loved to watch the light and shadow and colors around him and he learned how to

 capture them on paper and canvas. It was his favorite hobby, and he was quite good: he had won several prizes for his paintings in India. People especially liked the way he painted water scenes.

So, in 1896, after 25 years in India, he retired from Civil Service, he returned to England intending to devote himself to his painting, as well as raising his new family and writing down the insights and understandings he'd gathered in India. He had a decent pension from his years working for the government and a small inheritance from his parents that, he hoped, would support them until his writing and art might earn an income for them.

Whenever the weather allowed, he spent his days drawing and sketching the beautiful English country-side and coast. On rainy and icy days, he stayed inside and wrote. In the evening, after everyone else was asleep, he studied the big Bible he'd inherited from his mother—reading one Psalm every day and whatever else interested him.

In her foreword to one of the books that she helped publish after he had passed on, Annie Troward writes:

> When he retired from the Bengal Civil Service in 1896, he decided to devote himself to three objects -- the study of the Bible, writing his books, and painting pictures... He believed that the solution to all our problems was there (in the Bible) for those who read and meditated with minds at one with its Inspirer.[1]

Many times, she said, she would wake up in the middle of the night and find him on his knees in front of that big old Bible, deep in meditation and prayer.

---

[1] *Troward's Comments on the Psalms*

People who met Thomas in England described him as "homely"—a word that meant to them, "comfortable; feels like home." He was a kind and understanding man, simple and natural, who really enjoyed playing games with his children and thoughtfully guided them to be strong and happy adults. He took delight in each of their successes, and, as often as possible, he'd give them little sayings to help them remember the important things in life.

For example, when his son Rupert was drafted into the army at 17, a letter from his father offered a plan to succeed in all situations—a simple daily prayer, saying "Lord, let me find Thee this day in myself,"—after which, his father told him, he should "go forward in the full confidence that this prayer has been answered ... and," he said, "you will be surprised at how wonderfully it works." Not surprisingly, Rupert came home safely from the War.[2]

In a less profound but just as useful example, he would carefully move things aside as he passed things at the table, saying, "Two solid bodies cannot occupy

[2] This and all other quotes from letters from his children were taken from *Thomas Troward: An Intimate Memoir of the Teacher and the Man* by Harry Gaze.

the same space at the same moment of time, my dear."

He was also generous to others. His daughter Ruth said "I believe he never refused an alms (a charitable gift) to anyone who ever came to him in need." She told of how, one sad day, a window cleaner fell off a ladder while working at the Troward home. The man had come round every few weeks for some years so Thomas felt he knew him and did all he could to help. Ruth tells us he grieved deeply when the man died as a result of the accident. Then, since the man was unmarried and had no relatives, Thomas arranged and paid all the costs for his funeral and burial.

Thomas also loved to laugh and appreciated a good joke. He was good at puns, which he often made up at mealtimes with his family, and he sometimes played practical jokes with them. One of his favorites was to poke his head around the door of a room where his wife was absorbed in a book or a project and "meowing" loudly as if he were a cat demanding food. He would always chuckle when his wife jumped at the sound.

Thomas was near-sighted—so much so that without his glasses, he could not recognize anyone's face. His inability to see things clearly almost got him into serious trouble when England entered World War I. One fine day he picked up his sketching kit and headed out to the beaches as usual, not even seeing the signs telling people to stay away. Not until a Coast Guardsman came up and yelled at him that he'd almost been shot as a spy! Did he realize what he'd done?

4

A New Career

One day, Thomas was writing while waiting for his wife in a tea room near his new home in Norwood, then a suburb of London. He barely noticed when a lady happened to be seated at the same table, across from him. He was compiling some of his notes in his usual, large, clear, hand-writing, and she (being more curious than polite) couldn't help but read some.

As she later told the story, she was so surprised that she exclaimed, "Why sir, you really must pardon me for my apparent rudeness, but you wrote so large and so close to me I could not help seeing your words. What you are writing is Higher Thought or Divine Science, isn't it?"

"Why, madam, I trust that it really *is* higher thought, and certainly not lower thought," he replied.

"Well, I must explain my thoughtless interruption of your work. I am Mrs. Alice Callow, the secretary of a new organization at Kensington called the Higher Thought Center, where we study and listen to lectures on metaphysical Truth applied to health, spiritual unfoldment, and successful living." She continued, excitedly telling him that he really should visit them and perhaps lecture there.

And so began Thomas Troward's career as a lecturer and author.

This group welcomed him as a friend. He was invited to give short lectures and the Center, and soon after, in 1904, delivered what are now known as his famous Edinburgh Lectures at Queens Street Hall, near Queens Gate in Edinburgh, Scotland.

These lectures were delivered to very small but appreciative groups. They knew that what he had to say was brand new and wonderful, and that he was a well spoken and learned man.

Sadly, though, even this willing audience barely understood what he was saying. For, although he wrote well and was considered a very precise and proper Englishman with brilliant ideas, he was really boring as a speaker. He usually read his lectures in the monotone of the courtroom, instead of projecting his voice and sharing his enthusiasm as most public speakers do. And microphones had not yet been invented!

As one listener put it, "What little we heard was wonderfully good. Why don't you have it printed and published, so that we can get it all, and thoroughly understand it?"[3]

So it was that most of his audiences politely sat through his talk, then paid for it to be printed so they could read the book to find out what they'd missed while they were listening. How lucky for the rest of us that they did so!

A Preview of Future Attractions

In the days before that first lecture-series in Edinburgh, though, Thomas had an amazing experience. He later wrote about it in one of his books, *The Law and the Word:*

> Prior to my ever visiting Scotland at all—even before I had any idea that I ever would. I was wide awake, writing in my study at Norwood, when I suddenly seemed to be in a very different place, totally unknown to me. There stood the ruins of an ancient abbey, part of which still had some roof and was used

---

[3] *Thomas Troward, an Intimate Portrait,* by Harry Gaze, p. 50

for services. I was intrigued and, among other things, noticed an inscription in Latin on one of the walls. There seemed to be an invisible guide showing me around, who then pointed out a long low house opposite the abbey and said "this is the house of the clergyman of the abbey." Then I was guided into the house and shown a number of antique-looking rooms.

Just as suddenly I was once more only aware of sitting at my desk in my study, pen in hand. I had a clear memory of all I'd seen, but no idea where, or even if, it existed. I wrote the parts of the inscription that I remembered into a small note-book that I carry with me, thinking it might have some clue to explain the experience, and I would take the time to translate it at a later date.

Several weeks later I was invited to speak at Edinburgh and stayed in the home of one of the organizers of the lecture series. On the chance that maybe the place I had seen while sitting in my study was in Edinburgh, I showed my hostess and another guest the inscription I'd written in my notebook. Neither recognized it as being anywhere in the vicinity, so the experience was set aside as irrelevant.

I was invited to visit the home of the other guest on my way back to Norwood, which I did. She and her husband lived near Carlisle, and while I was there they showed me the beauties of the region, which include Lanercost Abbey. There, on one of the walls, was the inscription, which she also recognized as the one in my notebook. As I looked around, I realized that the place was exactly what I had seen during my experience sitting at my study desk. And there, across from it, was the long, low parsonage.

My hostess expressed disappointment that she didn't know the vicar, so we couldn't see the inside, and we turned to get into our carriage.

Just as we did so, however, a woman she did know, who happened to be the vicar's mother-in-law, came out of the parsonage and insisted we join her there for tea. Needless to say, the rooms of the home were very much as I had seen them in my earlier "tour."

Thomas shared another story in that same book. This one not only seemed to foretell the future, but also to witness someone else's decision-making process. It happened soon after he met Mrs. Callow.

> Some months earlier, when we had just moved into our home in Norwood, I was sitting at the dining table when suddenly I seemed to be standing in the hall. Two ladies passed very close to me and went on up the stairs, turning at the landing and continuing out of my sight. They looked as solid as anyone I've ever seen. One of them was stout, with a rosy complexion, wearing a silk blouse with thin purple and white strips. Leaning on her arm was a tiny little old lady dressed in black, with a lace mantilla.

> Then I was once again seated at my dining-room table, wondering what it all meant. Not wanting to alarm anyone I didn't tell my family members, but I did mention it to someone who had some experience with such matters. She said, matter-of-factly, "You have seen either someone who has lived in the house or who is going to live there."

> Almost a month later, my wife wrote a series of letters arranging for a governess to come live with us. The woman who arrived at our door was none other than the stout lady I had seen climbing the stairs—and arrived at breakfast the next morning wearing the very blouse I had seen.

> Not wanting to cause her any alarm, I waited six months before I felt we knew each

other well enough to dare broach the subject of the other woman I had seen with her. Finally, I found a suitable opportunity to ask if she knew anyone who fit that description.

Her look of surprise grew as I went on with my description. "Why, Mr. Troward, where could you have seen my mother? She is an invalid, and I am certain you have never seen her, and yet you nave described her most accurately!"

Then I told her what I'd seen. When she asked what I thought it could possibly mean, I replied that perhaps while she'd been looking for a post she had sent her thoughts to our place to see whether it would suit her and her mother had come along out of concern for her. Nothing more was said on the matter after that.

These stories, strange as they may seem, actually helped Thomas to make sense of the ideas he was trying to explain. They were his own, personal experience of what many people in India often talk about. A man from India named Yogananda wrote a book many years later called *Autobiography of a Yogi*[4] in which he describes both his father and himself meeting and talking with teachers who were later proven to have been sitting with an audience somewhere else at the time of those

---

[4] Paramahansa Yogananda, the founder of the Self-Realization Fellowship in the U.S.

meetings. It's interesting to note that Yogananda's experiences happened during the same years that Thomas was in India, not many miles away from where he lived and worked.

A Thought-form is Projected

Thomas had more such experiences as he continued writing and speaking. It was almost as if his constant prayer and determination to make his ideas clear opened up a whole new dimension for him.

> Some years later, I gave a second course of lectures in Edinburgh, but the friends I had stayed with the first time had moved away. Fortunately, a certain Mr. S invited me to stay with him for a day or two while I arranged something for the longer term. I had never seen his house, which was on the opposite side of town from where I had stayed before.

> When I arrived on a Tuesday, Mr. S and his family met me with the question, "What were you thinking of at ten o'clock on Sunday evening?" I didn't immediately remember, and wanted to know why they asked. "We have something curious to tell you," they replied, "but first try to remember what you were thinking about at ten o'clock Sunday evening— were you thinking about us?" Then I remembered that about that time I was in London, saying my usual prayers before going to bed and had asked that, if I could stay only a day or two with Mr. S, that I would be

guided to a suitable place for the remainder of my visit.

"That explains it," they replied. Then they went on to say that at that time Mr. S and his son, who was about twenty years old, had gone into the dining room together and had seen me standing, leaning against the mantel. As hard-headed Scotsmen who owned businesses in Edinburgh, they weren't the type to imagine such things, nor are they likely to both fantasize the same thing at the same time.

I can only suppose that they saw what they said they saw. I was not conscious of the "visit," so my only explanation is that in some way my thought had projected itself from London where I was praying, into that house in Scotland and made itself visible to them as the image of my body. I myself had no awareness of this process at all.

This experience, like the others Thomas shared in his books and talks, simply helped him understand more clearly who and what human beings are and how our minds affect matter. They showed him that regular, ordinary people can travel in time and see things in other places—and that they do it far more often than they realize.

5

Combining Science & Spirit

With all of his studies and all these experiences, Thomas was beginning to feel he had an explanation for how the world really worked. And, like many people who are trying to explain something that no one else has been able to, he used the most advanced science of his day for both a theory and a model of how it worked.

Radio had just been invented when Thomas and his family returned to England. While the telegraph had been in use for most of his career, the era of the wireless was just beginning.

Thomas kept track of all these new ideas because they helped him understand and explain the ideas he had been collecting.

He began to understand what many scientists now have proven: that all matter, in all its forms and across all space and time, is made up of the same stuff as energy. It's all tiny, vibrating particles of subatomic substance, very

far apart from each other, moving in waves across the universe. He understood that this one substance makes up everything in the universe.

Today physicists have called that substance "the quantum field," or "wavicles," and others have described it as the tips of "strings" that exist in more dimensions than our senses allow us to observe.

Regardless of what it's called, we perceive and name things by the differences: electrons and protons have different charges, negative and positive; living things are different from stones; and so on. But it's really all the same.

When this one substance acts through vibration, we measure it as waves. Radio and light waves travel through space; sound waves travel through air and water. We can drop a stone into water and observe the rings moving outward as waves, or see the way iron filings line up around a magnet. Telegraph operators generate electrical waves by means of sudden, sharp, electrical clicks in the Morse code. Radio does the same, but without the wires (Ham radio operators still learn and use Morse code). Computers send data bits as similar pulses on phone lines, cable wires, or fiber optics.

Thomas was particularly interested in something invented by Mrs. Watts-Hughes to demonstrate vibration. She called it an "eidophone" and it makes sand dance on the head of a drum when music is played near it. As the music stops, the sand settles into a pleasing pattern, often the shape of a tree or flower, but never a confused jumble; the music sets up an organized pattern of vibrations and the sand reveals that pattern. (There are YouTube videos on the shape of sound)

Thomas could see in all these examples that vibration patterns, as waves, always move out from an initial disturbance or action and have an impact on the world around them. He had learned that our brains and heart and lungs send out similar vibrations, too.

So he decided that our thoughts and feelings must send out patterns of vibration that affect the world around us. And, he reasoned, those vibrations are what made all his own amazing experiences happen.

One of the most interesting experiments he took part in used something called a "biometer" invented by a French scientist, Dr Hippolyte Baraduc.

The instrument consists of a bell glass [with a] a copper needle suspended by a fine silken thread [inside]. The glass stands on a wooden support, below which is a coil of copper wire which, however, is not connected with any battery or other apparatus, and merely serves to condense the current. Below the needle, inside the glass, there is a circular card divided into degrees to mark the action of the needle.

Two of these instruments are placed side by side, but in no way connected, and the experimenter then holds out the fingers of both hands to within about an inch of the glasses...

I approached the instrument in a very skeptical frame of mind; but I was soon convinced of my error. At first, holding a mental attitude of entire relaxation, I found that the left-hand needle was attracted through twenty degrees, while the right-hand needle, the one affected by the outgoing current, was repelled through ten degrees. After allowing the instrument to return to its normal equilibrium I again approached it with the purpose of seeing whether a change of mental attitude would in the least modify the flow of current. This time I assumed the strongest mental attitude I could with the intention of sending out a flow through the right hand, and the result as compared with the previous one was remarkable. The left-hand needle was now attracted through only ten degrees, while the right-hand one was deflected through something over thirty, thus clearly indicating the influence of the mental faculties in modifying the action of the current. I may mention that the experiment was made in the presence of two medical men who noted the movement of the needles.[5]

Then he found out that radio waves work best after the sun has set (ever turned on your a.m. radio after dark and listened to stations from other parts of the country?). So he figured that waves of thought or feelings must also work best after dark. That was how he explained why most people have "paranormal" or "psychic" experiences at night!

The more he worked to make sense of all the different kinds of things he studied and experienced, the more he realized that they all came from the same place. Just as matter and energy are one substance, he realized, all minds must be one mind.

---

[5] From *The Edinburgh Lectures, chapter 14.*

This one mind, he reasoned, is the basis for all of our individual minds, and is the source for all our sudden, great ideas. It isn't the part of our minds we're usually aware of—but it's there, all the time.

Through his studies and his experiments, Thomas figured out that when our thoughts and feelings are loving and joyful, they're vibrating in harmony with this one mind, and our lives are easy and good things just seem to happen for us. But when we're afraid or angry, our own thoughts and feelings are vibrating in a different way, and the kinds of things that happen seem distorted and uncomfortable.

He knew from all that he had learned in India that other people used other spiritual books and ideas to make their minds vibrate in harmony with the Universal Mind. For him, though, reading the Bible—especially the Psalms—was the best way to bring his thoughts into the universal vibration. So he read at least one psalm every day and closed his eyes and let the words sink in until he could feel them in his body.

6

The Word Spreads

Thomas began to write for a magazine called *Expressions*. This magazine sold in all English-speaking countries and as these articles sparked interest in his books, more were printed and selling well in both England and the U.S.

His most famous admirer in England was the priest in charge of Westminster Abbey, where the kings and queens of England are crowned. The priest's name was Archdeacon Wilberforce and he was well loved because he spoke so clearly about how God is Love and we are all an expression of God's love and have the Christ presence living in us. He also held a prayer service on Sunday evenings where many people were healed or had people they'd prayed for healed. More than all that, he had seen and heard many things like the strange things Thomas had. So it wasn't long before the two men became very close friends.

In the U.S., Thomas was making a big impact. William James, a Harvard philosopher whose work explaining religion was famous all over the world,[6] called Thomas' *Edinburgh Lectures* "far and away the ablest statement of philosophy I have met, beautiful in its sustained clearness of thought and style."

In Los Angeles a young man named Ernest Holmes found Thomas' books in a metaphysical library and was inspired to start teaching, which led to the formation of hundreds of Centers for Spiritual Living all over the world.

---

[6] James' most famous book is called *The Varieties of Religious Experience*, and in it he called New Thought, "the religion of healthy mindedness."

In New York a young British engineer named Emmet Fox, who grew up reading Troward's work, became a very popular minister and helped a man who called himself "Bill W" form an organization called Alcoholics Anonymous. That organization still helps millions of people discover their Higher Power and let go of their addictions.

Many, many others have been informed and comforted by the clear way that Thomas showed that science and spirituality work by the same laws. As a result, Thomas Troward became famous all over the world as the man who could make sense of what others hadn't been able to. He was able to show that the ancient religions said the same thing as modern science and that anyone who truly understood either must become a master of both—what a wonderful gift to us all!

Afterword

Thomas Troward was a quiet boy who had trouble in school. But he grew up to be an amazing man who managed to win respect as a British judge among the villagers of India, paint lovely seascapes that won prizes in both India and England, participate in and help others with very advanced experiments regarding mind and matter, lose one family to disease then raise a healthy family, and write almost a dozen books—some of which are still the best descriptions available of how mind and matter work together. What an amazing example he was of what we all can accomplish!

On May 16, 1916, at the age of 69, Thomas Troward passed from this plane. Yet even today, he influences people in the churches and schools of the New Thought Movement in the United States and Great Britain. He also, because of his close friendship and long correspondence with his good friend, Archdeacon Wilberforce of Westminster Abbey, led to some changes in the

Church of England (also called Anglican or Episcopal).

Yet this short, slender, thoughtful-looking man never thought of himself that way. In one of his books he says, "We must be like Peter Pan, the boy who never grew up—heaven defend me from ever feeling quite grown up; for then I shall come to a standstill."

Some of Thomas Troward's More Famous Books

- *The Edinburgh Lectures on Mental Science*

- *The Doré Lectures on Mental Science*

- *The Creative Process in the Individual*

- *Bible Mystery and Bible Meaning*

- *The Law and the Word*

- *The Hidden Power and Other Papers on Mental Science*

About the Author

Ruth L. Miller has spent her life integrating "the best of the past and present" for a more harmonious future. She has written several books about the history of or "metaphysical" religion in America. Her first book, *150 Years of Healing* introduces the founders and leaders of the New Thought movement. Her *Unveiling Your Hidden Power* explains the teachings of Emma Curtis Hopkins, the "teacher of teachers." The *Paths of Power* series are biographies of New Thought teachers for young readers.

Dr. Miller earned degrees in anthropology, cybernetics, environmental studies, and systems science, then worked as a futurist and professor before preparing for ordination as a minister in the New Thought tradition. In the process, she raised two daughters, one of whom is now a doctor and the other is a media producer.

About the Illustrator

Martha Shonkwiler is a retired school teacher, perpetual student, and a grandmother. After a career as a teacher, she studied "Healing through Art and Spirituality," receiving three theological seminary and university degrees. Then she volunteered for six years as a chaplain, labyrinth facilitator, art therapist and "Healing Touch" practitioner at the hospital in Grants Pass, Oregon, where she lives in the beautiful woods.

Her focus now is relaxing, creating art, and enjoying her grandchildren (and children) with nature walks, art, and travel adventures. Martha appreciates the Grants Pass Center for Spiritual Living.

WiseWoman Press
Vancouver Washington
800.603.3005

The Paths of Power series:

- *A Power Beyond Magic:* The Extraordinary Life of Ernest Holmes'
- *The Power of Unity:* The Amazing Discoveries of Charles Fillmore
- *Power to Heal:* The mystical life of Emma Curtis Hopkins
- *The Power of Mind:* Phineas Quimby finds a New Thought

Also by Ruth L. Miller

Unveiling Your Hidden Power: Emma Curtis Hopkins' Metaphysics for the 21st Century

> (a text with the lessons and commentary, a Workbook with daily practices for the 12 lessons, and "The Class" a guide for facilitators)

Coming into Freedom: Emilie Cady's Lessons in Truth for the 21st Century

Spiritual Success: A Guide for Daily Practice

www.wisewomanpress.com

Paths of Power

Boys and girls and men and women all over the world have found a kind of power that transforms lives. These are their stories— how they found the power, what they did with it, and how their own lives were transformed in the process.

This kind of power is greater than magic, because it transforms, rather than just changing any appearances. This power is, as one great teacher said, "more than supernatural; it is supremely natural."

The *Paths of Power* series tells the stories of those who've gone before so that new generations will discover and use these remarkably human, God-given abilities.